Often in Different Landscapes

The University of Texas Press Poetry Series, No. 1

Often in Different Landscapes

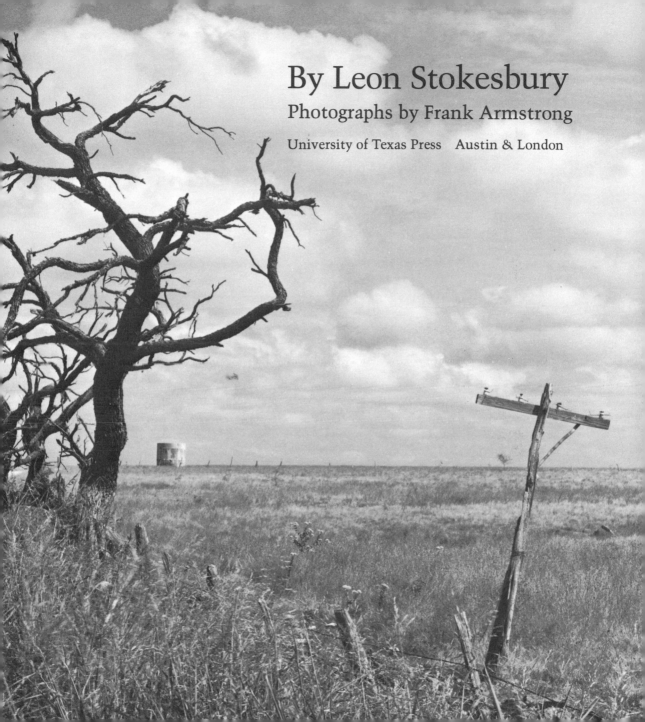

By Leon Stokesbury

Photographs by Frank Armstrong

University of Texas Press   Austin & London

Library of Congress Cataloging in
Publication Data
Stokesbury, Leon, 1945–
    Often in different landscapes.
    (The University of Texas Press
poetry series; no. 1)
    I. Armstrong, Frank, 1935– II. Title.
PS3569.T6223O35   811'.5'4   76–16478
ISBN 0–292–76004–3
ISBN 0–292–76005–1 pbk.

Grateful acknowledgment is made for permission to
    publish the following poems:
"Aesthetic Distances." *The New Orleans Review* 2,
    no. 2 (1970). "Poem." *The New Orleans Review*,
    forthcoming (1976). By permission of *The New
    Orleans Review*.
"Back Behind the Eyes," "The Graduate Assistant
    Tells about His Visit," "Little Keats' Soliloquy,"
    "To Laura Phelan: 1880–1906," "Summer in
    Fairbanks." In *New Voices in American Poetry*,
    ed. David Allan Evans. Cambridge, Mass.:
    Winthrop Publishers, 1973.
"Back Behind the Eyes," "Summer in Fairbanks,"
    "The True Meaning of Life Revealed." *Prairie
    Schooner* 14, no. 3 (Fall 1971). Reprinted from
    Prairie Schooner by permission. Copyright ©
    1971 by the University of Nebraska Press.
"Beef," "The Man Who Distributes the Fever
    Blister Ointment," "Mammoth Poem," "Written
    in the Fall." *The Carolina Quarterly* 22, no. 1
    (Winter 1970).
"But Once in Special." *Poetry Northwest*, 14, no. 1
    (Spring 1973).
"California." *Poem*, nos. 3 and 4 (Summer and Fall
    1969).
"Clever Hans," "On the Comeback Trail." *Poetry
    Now* 3, no. 2 (Spring 1976).
"Concern," "What It Feels Like to Live in This
    Country to Me." *Quartet Magazine* 6, nos. 42–
    43 (Spring–Summer 1973).
"The Death of Harpo Marx." *Three Sisters* 1, no. 2
    (Winter 1972).

"Footlight Parade," "In a Cold Country," "Often in
    Different Landscapes." *The Mill Mountain Re-
    view* 2, no. 2 (Winter 1975).
"Gifts," "The North Slope." In *Eating the Menu:
    A Contemporary American Poetry, 1970–1974*.
    Dubuque, Iowa: Kendall/Hunt Publishing Co.,
    1974.
"The Graduate Assistant Tells about His Visit,"
    "Little Keats' Soliloquy." *Shenandoah* 22, no. 3
    (Spring 1971).
"The Lamar Tech Football Team Has Won Its
    Game." *The New Yorker*, October 21, 1967. "The
    Lamar Tech Football Team Has Won Its Game,"
    © 1967 The New Yorker Magazine, Inc.
"Looking for It," "Why I Find Myself Immersed in
    Few Traditions." In *The New Breed: An Anthol-
    ogy of Texas Poets*, copyright 1973, Prickly Pear
    Press, permission to reprint by Dave Oliphant,
    Editor.
"The Poet on Personal Divinity." In *Intro 4*, ed.
    Walton Beacham and R. V. Cassill. Charlottes-
    ville: University Press of Virginia, 1972.
"The Polar Bear" originally appeared in *Intro 2*,
    edited by R. V. Cassill; copyright © 1969 by
    Bantam Books, Inc. Reprinted by permission of
    the publisher.
"Scorpio," "To His Book." *Red Weather* 1, no. 1
    (Summer 1976).
"Song of the Incredible Lonzo." *Stone Drum* 2 (Fall
    1972).
"Summer in Fairbanks," "To Laura Phelan: 1880–
    1906." In *Best Poems of 1971: Borestone Moun-
    tain Poetry Awards*, vol. 24. Palo Alto, Calif.:
    Pacific Books, 1972.
"To Laura Phelan: 1880–1906." In *New Southern
    Poets*, ed. Guy Owen and Mary C. Williams.
    Chapel Hill: University of North Carolina Press,
    1974.
"To Laura Phelan: 1880–1906," "To All Those
    Considering Coming to Fayetteville." *Southern
    Poetry Review* 12, no. 1 (Fall 1971).
"What the New Chef Said." *Lowlands Review* 1,
    no. 1 (Spring 1975).

If this is tea, please bring me some coffee.
If this is coffee, please bring me some tea.

— ABRAHAM LINCOLN

Contents

Often in Different Landscapes

Little Keats' Soliloquy

You're probably wondering
what I'm doing with this
2-by-4 said a stable boy,
and when I came to with
dried blood in my ear
I knew that I had
missed the joke again.
It happens all the time:
that was no refried banana
that was my wife. That
means something? Meant nothing
to me while they grinned
their asses off. You go
straight to hell I said;
but I can't go through
life this way, always outside
watching the baker
plopping pastries into
sacks for other kids,
that's no good, I know
that for sure, but what
can I do, what can I
use for a ladder, what
to carry me up into
the loft, away from these
stinking horses?

Most people, of which I am
one, look upon themselves as
more or less experts about
being alone, loneliness,
large holes, etc., but
when, on a recent visit
to my great aunt, she told me
she had been writing quite long
letters for several years
to Lucky, her dead dog, I was
taken by surprise. Also
she said, "Now honey, I want
you to remember always
to keep your writing on the
highest level." I had sent
her a copy of a small
anthology in which I
did not cuss. I guess that was
what she meant. She seemed proud
of that; then, when I took her
out to eat at this Italian
place, the sky writers were
on the job, telling us to
go somewhere else. Well, she liked
the pepperoni pizza
OK, saying only, "There
really isn't too much here
for the price you have to pay."
I drank to that. Once again
outside, we saw the writing

on the sky had rotted all
away. Twilight was coming.
Already in the alleys
and clogging up the sewers
some fistulas of darkness
were floating around. And so
when I left her that evening
she kissed me on the cheek, then
took her handkerchief and wiped
the lipstick off. After which
miles fell between us. My aunt
is old, and she never went
to college. And so, I
think she knows, perhaps, nothing
or at the most very little
probably, of irony,
or of ambiguities,
or of anything that is
anything at all like that.

The Murder of Gonzago and His Friends

In a district that's rarely traveled these days,
in a place where even the blackbirds lie down
in daylight, just north of Anadarko,
I fell out with eight debauchees below some sycamores.
"Good fellows, arise!" I cried. "I
imagine you have heard the sad news."
But they were dull, sluggard, adamant, insane.
And besides, Mogen David seemed their chief concern.
The Arapahoes would soon be upon us: "Arise! Arise!
Shall blood-purple be the color of our pain?"
Nothing. Their eyes were not white rapids.
But no one could say I did not try. No one felt
I was to blame. No one. This was many years ago.
At night now, when I leave the house
with my jar of salt, my thoughts are of them. Each night
as I stand under my streetlight, I can think
only of them. And as I look down the long row
of streetlights, each with its own person,
holding his own jar, as I stand there
pouring salt on the slugs, that then blister and foam,
as I watch them dissolve, my thoughts are always of them.

Beef

When the fat woman's two brats
went with their noses running
toward the wrong Steak House rest-
room door, her husband laughed and laughed
and caught them just in time. He
stopped them, set them straight, then
came back grinning, saying "Well
they're safe for a few more years."
He steered them a proper course
toward a proper watered harbor,
safe from strange equipment
and stranger squalls and thighs. He grinned. He
slashed and tore broiled steak. He
wolfed down dark red catsup with his french fries

Back Behind the Eyes

In this poem I am fast asleep in bed.
Over my head, there floats
a large and white oval bubble, in which
can be seen, not a log being sawed
by a saw, but instead, two people
familiar to me. They are turning to me
now and, yes, I have often seen them before.
It is a bare scene, frayed and vague
near the sides; but there is definitely
a door towards the back. And also towards the back
is a bed in which a small boy lies asleep.
The bubble over his head contains
a tiny chain saw that whines softly and whirrs.
Both parents say bitter things and wave
their arms vigorously. The upper lip
of each curls back revealing the obscene
pinkness of moist gums. And occasionally,
the mother cries and menstruates. Lightly,
lightly. Odors of shrimp. They take turns
exiting out the door in the back. While one
is gone, the other walks to the bed, picks up
the child, and always whispers in its ear.
The boy, wearing only underwear, and with
a birthmark on his thigh, listens to each parent
then sobs and sobs. This scene is repeated
perhaps twenty times. Sometimes the father
carries a bag of golf clubs with him
as he goes. Usually not. For many nights now
all this has recurred. It is, I suppose, a habit

to be quickly wakened from. And I will be.
I know that soon I will rise from this poem,
and sit up in bed, looking over the side
as always, at the tops of my empty shoes,
two dark mouths opened, rightly, in horror
at what they are being asked to sustain.

What should be done? No one knew for sure.
"Look at that chili-dog," I said to the blind guy,
after which I took it on the lam. The entire
offended countryside was up in arms. *The Scourge
of Sheboygan* the media labeled me. Those swine,
they forced me to the forests, taking shelter
in an abandoned hunting lodge. And only sometimes,
on the weekends, would I hear the snickering sounds
of couples in the woods. That first night, that
lonely night, the sleep dripped from my eyes,
was replaced by more, and rain dripped, and the dark
with its hard tonnage, I should add, also dripped,
oozing like hot asphalt under the door. Why
did it remind me so much of the blind guy
and his constant drool? My gorge rose. But not
for long. I packed those days with simple things,
taking up the Ace comb with cellophane, playing
songs of my own invention, such as "Johnny Belinda
Where is Thy Sting," a personal favorite. But that, too,
sometimes brought thoughts of the blind guy, why
I don't know. And neither do I understand
where these recurring images come from, strange
images, often in different landscapes, and always
coming back, huge indigestions, to glut
my sleep, my waking moments, all my life
clogged with glossolalia, white canes, shrieks, slobber,
the spastic I tripped once behind the gym.

The True Meaning of Life Revealed

Some personage is at this very minute driving across
the well-worn plains. Who do you suppose it is?
He arrives, smiling; making awkward apologies
for his Ford's disarray. Do you think this means
you're to join him in his travels? He doesn't say.
Oh, and you were just getting ready to think about
your first love for the first time in years.
Here come five clouds, shrugging along. Notice
how they hover and begin to rain. This all seems
connected, but he continues simply smiling, his moustache
aquiver, and hands you the envelope, that you cannot open,
in which, he claims, is concealed his mission and name.

Footlight Parade

A short man was excited. He wanted to put on
a show. Women were dancing. He was excited.
People ran around. A blonde woman liked him. But
he didn't know it. He liked another woman.
Well, he got drunk. He wasn't supposed to though.
Women were dancing. They were singing. Then, the blonde
woman saved him. He talked fast. He was excited.
Some other things happened. He put on the show.
Another man and woman sang in it. She was
so pretty. They were in a big hotel. It was called
Honeymoon Hotel. They sang in the hotel. They sang
in the halls. More people came and sang. The man
and woman went to bed and sang. That was the end
of that show. Well, then the man who sang asked
the woman who sang to marry him. She said she would.
He kissed her. They they put on another show. The man
and woman sang again. Then a lot of women swam.
They were happy. They swam. They were pretty. Then
that was the end of that show. Then they went
and put on another show. The first man got in a fight.
Then he danced and sang. He was a sailor then.
After that show was over, he asked the blonde woman
to marry him. She smiled. She said she would.

Concern

The one who conceived of the world
as a still pool in the street
and now in that pool of still water
several dark colors move in thick turgid swirls
The one who upon our first encounter
confided to me that the night was not the night
but was actually dirt and she had often been soiled
The one who upon our first encounter
was standing under the shadow of two crows in a tree
The one whose lashes were rows of black reeds
or were they oars rowing
the deep galleys of her eyes back from Troy
The one whose muscles were sachets of fear
The one whose scream was the ripping of a red towel
The one whose nipples were burgundy stars
The one who burns

But Once in Special

Get out of here with your ideas about
going downtown to see that roller coaster
and no I do not want to buy any more
ping pong balls now look this is my room
I pay the rent so please remove
these midgets and try to understand
it's nothing personal actually I've
always liked shorter Get away from that
aquarium if you don't mind God damn
people this is well OK see it was
the other day or maybe last year
I don't remember too clearly any more
I slid into this out of sight witch
her dark eyes sadder than the sea
try to understand when she moved the air
flowed out in waves before her and she moved
so softly those waves they still keep rolling over me

Gifts

They say that blood is salt. I've
tasted yours, and they are right.
So let's get on with our big painting
exchange. In mine, I've placed you
in a black pasture, with black horses,
your red eyes clearly discerned. But,
and I observe you're having the same
problem, here in the middle distance
isn't really the right place for you
somehow. Over more to the left,
I think, yes, under that smeared vision
of crows, way out in those dark, waist-high
weeds, there, leaning against that
huge pile of horseshit, yes, and a little
nearer the vanishing point, thank you.

The Poet on Personal Divinity

Occasionally, I've thought it would be good
to fix the world. Just last week, I saw
a man with his brain splattered all over
the road. The brain is not grey, as many
think, but more a pinkish with streaks of white
and red. Or maybe that was just the mess;
who could tell? Anyway, in Oklahoma City
a man who built a one-mile-square-housing-
addition explained they were all alike, except
"the garage and bathrooms, which are switched around
so people won't think they're all the same." And
Alice, married to Tom, cried late one night
"I love him but I think he hates my guts!" At which
I got out of bed to take a leak. Christ. And I would try
to fix all this; set my sign in the stars, so to speak. If
only it weren't so long it's been this way.
So many centuries it keeps just hanging here,
a dark shirt in a black closet,
waiting forever for something to fill it up.

On the Walk

You coming down the walk,
You that I know
Don't look too soon. I
Caught you looking from
Far off, and how you jerked
Your eyes to grass, and
Trees, and then your
Own feet.

Then, when we almost meet,
It seems that I look
Better than your feet.

The Lamar Tech Football Team Has Won Its Game

The Lamar Tech football team has won its game.
My grandmother has died. The newspaper, yesterday,
Said, "Siamese Twins Cut Apart, One Lives." My father
Says, "Some things you have to learn to accept.
Take the good parts with the bad."
                              (This must be a dream.)
"Oh, yes," I say. "I remember how the sun feels warm
Even on the coldest days, sometimes."
The Lamar Tech football team.   The newspaper.

Belgium is now importing jukeboxes.
Australians are installing oil heaters.
Adversity is what makes you mature. "Oh, yes.
I've seen the winter moon pumped up, platinum-like;
And the stars seem brightest when it's freezing."
Siamese twins.   On the coldest days, sometimes.
                              (This must be a dream.)
My father says, "Make hay while the sun shines."
The sun.   The moon.   Belgium is now importing
Jukeboxes.   One lives.   My father says, "In a few weeks
You'll feel better. Time is a great healer."   The sun.
The moon.
The Lamar Tech football team has won its game.

In a Cold Country

It was such a very grey day that the clouds
would not hold; letting go snowflakes at graveside
to stick to black dresses, plastic grass, and
the white or purple wreaths propped all around.
Later, the gathering showed a kitchen table
stuffed with pies. Someone fixed me up, and soon
my mouth was full, so I couldn't join in
the many conversations at my side. Pecan
pie filling between my teeth. My parents
knew I was upset. My father took me
for a drive down by the river, where we parked
and sat, and talked of several things: I don't
recall of what exactly, for this is all
wrapped in thick cotton. But I do remember
one thing, and that because my father
has told me of it since. When the talk lulled,
I felt very cold; and staring out the window
for a minute or two, I turned, and asked
my father to look out on the river.
So we sat there for some time, not saying
any more, but just watching the snowflakes
and what happened when they fell there.

Why I Find Myself Immersed in Few Traditions

So what if the world needed potatoes.
Columbus could have lied when he went back.
Too easily satisfied, those chocolate eyes
of the native girls were slanted enough for him.
It isn't his fault really. How could he have
foreseen these orange arroyos where the people
come to dream of sleep? I'm here right now,
and I can barely believe it myself:
the hot nights, the brown trees making
the insane clicking sounds of a hundred cicadas,
these numerous dry and vaguely heart-shaped rocks.
Now so what if an after-dinner smoke
is nice. What's that when you can't tell
the moon from the streetlights. And even when you can
it looks covered with lint. Oh sure, we and everything
keep going on and on. But let me tell you,
when our caryatids start crumbling,
and when we wait in our western airports
longing for tickets to non-existent lands,
our luggage heavy with a few big books,
then, buddy, it makes it pretty damned hard
to lean on the past, when you see all this as just
the final end of a lot of peristalsis.

At My Great Aunt's

This was my home when I was three and four.
Nothing's ever changed here. Nothing. Never.
Odd furniture, the parlor and dark mirror,
The dusty fake ferns drooping like dead feathers.
And here's a color portrait of myself:
Smiling, cute and small, with coat and tie on.
Beside it, a ball rests on the shelf,
Belonging to her poodle twelve years gone.

And after we have left, my aunt will sit
And watch the sunset strike her chandelier
That throws a hundred rainbows on the wall.
Those rainbows then will fade, and then grow faint,
And finally each run down into a blur,
Then out of sight somewhere, beyond recall.

Clever Hans

In the lower left-hand corner and nude
it is a beige room with a beige floor cold
nothing else but a set of freshman themes
Robert Hollyfield before me whispering
the brain have no use anymore
it is just a beige room with a beige floor
no need for this cold but I remember when
she did not forgive me for thirty-five days
I beat my fist on the bed and soon I
was buying lubricants in Morris Pharmacy
again ah if only I could talk with Kathy
or the President about the refusal of
the American people to perceive irony
but I haven't seen either for years besides
what could I ever say to her after
that time I puked all over her mother's
brand new dinette set I was so ashamed
Christ things haven't been the same since
the day the big-time poet cackled my efforts
were obscene Turd I thought cow fadookie
we were sitting by the motel pool I
remember then that granite brow gazed up
exclaiming Oh my look an eagle soaring
Jesus Christ man it was a buzzard but I held
my tongue for the grand old boy now what
is that it is disgust and fear obscene
obscene then as everything went dark and when
the screen lit up there's Fat Sally Rodríguez
walking along the freeway wanting to sell

some relics but along chugs Chester A.
Arthur in his Dodge his muttonchops
blowing in the breeze she espied those chops
you know the rest a dirt road pine branches
slapping the windows as they drive along stop
her hand on his crotch then the knife into her
over and over and disembowelment guts
sliding onto the floor the dark flow and
tan stitching on the tan vinyl seat-
covers acquiring a permanent stain
Oh the irony of it we scream and scream
but obscene how how how isn't it only
just a beige room with a beige floor where
at one end a funny man has forgotten
his funny clothes so shakes then settles down
to read the words of the illiterate again

A Light Green Lawn

If I have created the crow,
Walking there, on the light green lawn,
In front of this front porch—

And, even if I did not create
The twilight now lumbering, also,
Across this lawn—

And, I did create that crow, I think,
It hatched from my head, fluttered
Above me, settling out on the green—

Shall it then squawk, strut, in front of me,
Vaudevillian, thumb to its nose, and, on its own
Spit back the always "Unending!" It

Which can shake, shake its ebony wing,
Be above everything, and,
Blot out the sun of its own accord?

Well, the bird is out now. Shall I let it
Continue its dance into dark?
I think not. I think, rather,

To construct now a knife. Reach out
For the bird. Cut it. Cut it. Until
The night's final fumbling across this lawn.

What It Feels Like to Live in This Country to Me

Where are all those yucks? With a more silent nature
than that of the corpse's fingernail stretching out
on the silk, up from the sea of stone, the sea
from which thought does not arise, an emotion
is headed our way. And speaking of fingernails,
I saw a movie once where they buried this guy
alive, because they thought he was dead. He wasn't. Later,
they dug him up and he was. Fingernails, stubs, had raked
that coffin lid until it was streaked, smeared. He
wanted out, see. What could be more plain? Ah, now,
the guiding light is followed by the edge of night,
has been for years, and this experience, myself,
me and the television I'm observing at this
very minute, Bob Hope, with the sound off, bid a fond
farewell, to paraphrase Rilke somewhat loosely,
from the ballroom of the ambiguously blessed, and
O those cards and O those letters, communication,
reason is where it's at, but, as I said
with considerable power, in another poem
of my own making, Where is it?, who knows,
and to be quite honest, who gives a shit, what did I
just say?, Huntz Hall be with me till I end my song,
the log has been flogged behind the grey barn now,
out there, where snow is embraced gently by the earth,
where the earth is soaked from all that embracing, where
there is only a speck left, that's where it's at
after all, yes sir, just a dot, a raft at sea,
undefined, no distinguishing marks, the last placebo,
fading away like a stain into the realms of rue.

Poem

In this print of Dürer's hanging on the wall
The knight and horse are old but very strong;
The lines run down his face, his body clothed
Completely in thick armor that he loves.
His friend, a dog, runs gladly at his heel,
And they'll crush skulls before the day is gone.
Behind him, loom monsters and monstrosities
That he's absorbed, or beaten, either way.

And Death arrives. His face sits on his sleeve,
An hourglass in his hand. The knight—
Is not afraid. No doubt he knows his way.
And there, see, on a hill, the furthest thing
Away, already passed, but visible, stand
The towers of a town where peace might be.

Looking for It

He could sense it deep,
running through the October
leaf snows that were starting
to drift down. Colors of blood
were the maple leaves. But see,
it was like the last pickle
in the jar when your fork
is too short: swimming around,
skitting away out of reach.
And it was the same when he
walked the grey beach. Rough,
rough at the shore roared the thick sea,
but this faint chattering of
a million monkeys, herds of
monkeys behind the sand dunes
somewhere, was always not there
when he went to see. He just
could not get at it, though he
tried and tried. At night the usual
stars flicked on, leaving long black
absences filling most of
the sky. He studied, studied,
but he never could read what
the wind was saying when it came
muttering through the many-
fingered trees, sifting far down
through the leaves such a thin sound
of fierce and senseless surgery.

Aesthetic Distances

From the second balcony
Hamlet was a black stumbling ant
or mote of dust swirled in white
footlights, or perhaps any asking
and quick indistinguishable thing
very like a quail flapping fast
out in front of your car spilling
from its mouth small sounds.

What the New Chef Said

"Those tapioca-type idiots
who come in here expecting
some kind of lethargic lull
to fill their puffed-out paunches
had damn better lift
their lardy asses up
and right on out the door. If
they hang long around here
I'll take a skewer
and stick the hogs, rotten
or not. What they want
is the old way, the old slow
metronome of flavors chopped
out and dropped on a plate
to set before the dunce.
That's over! All over!
Today's green salads
are the truly tossed
with sundry graffiti of zucchini
and weenie and bologna sprinkled
over all. I give the people
what the world is really like:
strawberry buttermilk
and prune pie. Ice
creams lost in sauerkraut.
That sweet-and-sour sauce
is what I make and
what I make is what (though
it bust their ulcerous guts)
what they devour!" he said.

Religious Poem

I wandered another sadness off
in Shakespearean dusk in November.
Sad images. Bone trees, and so on.
Let my many gargoyle faces come whirling!
Oh, which to choose. Shall it be Paul Scofield
as Thomas More? Jesus no! Or how about
Jesus? That's one I've done. Of course I
never admitted it was Jesus; and often
I would change the appearance, so it looked like
someone besides Jesus. After all, if
people saw a person going around with
the face of Jesus on, well, that would be
a little self-indulgent. I mean, Jesus
is a deity and everything; some people
might see it as a sacrilege. Anyone might.
You have to be real careful. I
argued with myself, and so on, and on.

Song of the Incredible Lonzo

Thick hours lie like braces and the tang
of quite a few daiquiris collects around
the yellow bottoms of the tongues of Sue
and Shirley yanking fishsticks from the stove O
and ah my sweet Jesus is it not at this time
in the cool of the evening in the cool
of the day usually an old girl's fancy
turns to thoughts now of the incredible Lonzo
crawling over the backyard fence or maybe
up the drain or coming God from somewhere
importantly unexpected but never the clothes hamper
with its white shirts' ballpoint pens left in
in darkness as now on comes Lonzo the fair
the magnificent Lonzo that wild one she cries
salty sweat making muscles glisten in
the sun the sweet salad of his hair blowing
she cries O and again O and Lonzo my
beloved may might must can could the quick
brown fox this this at last is given unto me
as into the room roar those strangers her
own children her fine children her very own
white rabbits of the night demanding mayonnaise

The Man Who Distributes the Fever Blister Ointment

The man who distributes the fever blister ointment
Is truly my hero.

He lives next door.
It is he who knows
All the sensitive regions
Where the ointment must go.
                        Late at night
He gets phone calls from people who ask him,
"Come." And he goes.

To be sure, like him, of that company map
Showing which dark country, or steaming zone
Is the place where skins swell fevered with pulp,
Soft sacs expanding, rich heat roaring in—

To be sure, to be sure, under what boiling sky.

Each evening I meet him on his way to work.

Each evening he's laughing, looks back waving,
Good-bye, good-bye.

Written in the Fall

The thick book grows heavy,
a slab of bad meat
in my hand. I lean back
closing my eyes; I can hear
the faint clang my heart makes
there, and there, there, and
on as it strikes the deep
bars of my chest. Outside,
long leaves float down like
abandoned rowboats dropping
over the falls. The ad men
stand knocking at the front
door now; while the clock starts
its whirring, its hands black
propellers beginning to spin,
to spin. The book pages
flop over, splashing grease
on my arms, being blown
by that wind. The dark
ad men are coming on in.
I cannot stop them.
The fat book falls.
The wind is rushing.
And they carry huge stones
in those hands.

The Gold Rush

Let us enter pursued by a bear.
   The balmy lord doffs
his derby. Snow swirls everywhere.
   Always the cold, always
the stumbling from place to small place

to shut out the meanings of
   snow for a while.
Tied to a dog that drags us
   from grace, remember
the night he opened his door

and a mule walked in. Then we were
   the one, the acquaintance
forgot, the face of despair,
   tottering there on that
distant cliff. Snow swirls everywhere.

The Zany

Once upon a time we were all sitting around in the tomb
after supper when this guy comes to the door
dressed in the skin of one of those animals
that swore they would never die and introduced himself
as certainly the new Midas for our times
and so he says to us he says

watch me

Glory he made the prongs of a pitchfork glow
Glory he fried an egg in his palm
Glory he touched books and the books burned
and then he finished
by reaching for the one he said he loved

Tears would pool
then sizzle down each flushed cheek and away

Wow

I was impressed

My name
by the way
is The Wild Bull of the Pampas

Here comes
The Wild Bull of the Pampas
people often say

Beautiful

But now I feel I know
what the new Midas meant when
he spoke of a weariness
at hearing
each time
the titty pink applause
of various groups
who screamed Lawzee
and such

somehow

There was this traveling salesman
see who stopped for the night
at the home of this farmer
who had two really fine daughters
and a prize milk cow oh yeah

But that isn't what I wanted to say

And neither was that

and so forth

and so on

These birds in the trees
these leaves in the trees
these pale flowers in the grass I mow
these remind me now
of cosmologies not my own

And the arms tire

And the heart tires

And the song slows down
to the wrong speed

Which reminds me
of this jukebox
see
in Burkeville Texas
which would play
if you punched C-6
a record supplied by the Ku Klux Klan
which went
Move them niggers north boys
Move them niggers north
If they don't like our southern ways
Move them niggers north oh yeah

No

That isn't it

That isn't what I wanted to say

somehow

I think
I wanted to say something
about when the odors of leaves
would return to these voices

about when I could talk about
the children again

about when I can walk there
in the high grass
where the beast grazes
at ease
with a quiet strength
waiting to engender
and join a slow
a soft falling into
the pool
of the peace

of this earth

yeah

that
is a little like
something I wanted to say

The Death of Harpo Marx

It was the summer of dutchmen
  who painted the stars
Of fleas and of plague
  and magistrates closing
  theaters down
The summer of copper
  at the center of dimes
It was the summer they ran
  the sad Jew out of Spain
Of screaming and scratching
  at Chuck Berry's big
  rock-and-roll review
The summer the Kansans
  made some money
Of telling why
  dead trees grow
Of niggers advancing
  from the Adirondacks
The summer he had
  nothing more to say

On the Comeback Trail

The sad-eyed riders of the purple sage
are burning ranches out along
the foggy distant northern borders.
It was they who took the complete works
of Winslow Homer off into the hills.
They burned them. Lord, the flakes and pigments
fell for days from those mile-high haciendas.
Word came that several halfway houses
were smoulders too. And so. That settled it.
Leaving behind even Miss Eikenhorst, bright braces
glinting up her smiles; leaving behind
an unspoken, alas, passion for said fine freshman
remedial English student; leaving
dumplings behind, this dude:
me: myself: I: simply just left town.
The rest of this poem will be in the first person.
I don't know how I did it. The way
was long. With Mortimer Ennis, my only
constant companion, I strove. But even he
fell away, tempted by weirdnesses
at the outer provinces. How in the hard times
the weak do wash away! Strange.
At last, to have reached these windows. And now. Now
simply step out. "Simply" was the word all along.
There. Done. So. Isn't that a song playing somewhere?
I think . . . Yes. It is. It is "Never No More
Blues." Wait. Wait. No, it is "Moonlight and Skies."

To Laura Phelan: 1880–1906

for Jim Whitehead

Drunk I have been. And drunk I was that night
I lugged your stone across the other graves,
to set you up a hundred yards away.
Flowers I found, then. Drunk I have been.
And am, standing here with no moon to spill
on the letters of your name; my loud fingers
feeling them out. The stone is mossed over.
And why must I bring myself in the dark
to stand here among the sour grasses
that stain my white jeans? Drunk I have been.
See, the thick dew slides on the trees, wet weeds,
wetness smears the air; and a vague surf
of wildflowers pushes my feet, slipping
close to my legs. When the thought comes at last
that people fall apart, that the things we do
will not do. Ends. Then, we come to scenes
like this. This scene of you. You apart:
this is not you; and yet, this is where I stand
and close my eyes, and feel the ragged wind
blow red and maul my hair. In the night somewhere,
dandelions foam. This is not you. Drunk
I have been. Across this graveyard, that
is where you are. Yet I stand here. Would ask
things of your name. Would wish. Would not be told
of the stink in the skull, the eye's collapse.
Would be told something new, something unknown.—
A mosquito bites my hand. The only sound
is the rough wind. Drunk I have been,
here, at the loam's maw, before this stone
of yours, which is not you. Which is.

Scorpio

Pendant, hanging from a golden chain,
    Go to this woman now.
Miles from here, when you were made,
    A man's hand fashioned you
In fire, until a golden dew of sweat
Was on you both. And here you rest
    An intricate detail
In a soft sway. Go to this woman now.

Guard her. Keep her from harm.
    Float there, above her breasts,
So near her heart, your barb upraised
    To any who might hurt
That great fragility. O ancient
And most strange, of all the signs,
    Glow, shine, blaze out for her
Her path among these often-freezing stars.

Yes. But sometimes, when one man comes near,
    If she should smile, drop down
Your guard, that she might know, so she
    Might feel, that here is one
Who sees the sun and moon in her,
Because the sun and moon are there,
Who, when she walks, can hear
The chimes inside his own breast ring,
Who loves her, and drifts within her
Only to love her, who wants always to touch
    Her lips, to take and give
This flooding, gentle, kind, and complex sting.

East Texas

The taste in my mouth
Was the taste of blood or rust on backdoor thermometers
Unread for twenty years. With my cheesecloth
Net I waited in the woods. Then the flutters
Of the giant swallowtails could be heard far away. Leaves
Moved. Sweat was acid in my eyes, and my father frowned
In his huge wheelchair. He could not get up the hill. My last two loves
But one sat in pine straw, waiting to see what I would do. The sound
To my left was the sound of men standing at urinals.
But no. It was only the rain, uncontrollable, and the rain took
The grey shapes of steam. My father frowned. It was so steep.
And those shapes were the shapes of old women with shawls
On their heads, of old men sitting down. She shook
Me saying I was talking in my sleep.

To All Those Considering Coming to Fayetteville

Often these days, when my mind holds splinters
like the pieces of the shampoo bottle
I dropped and shattered yesterday, I think
of other places. It is wintertime now,
and the Ozarks are hushed up with snow
everywhere. They are small mountains, almost
not mountains at all, but rather, with trees
sticking up, they seem more like
the white hairy bellies of fat old men
who have lain down here. What has this to do
with anything? I don't know. Except
it makes me think of snow elsewhere, and what
it would be like to be there. I might drive
across Oklahoma, then on into
New Mexico. I could be there tonight.
The land would be flat, the snow over
everything. The highway straight, and forever
the snow like blue cheese in the moonlight,
for as far as there is, and air, cold air
crisp as lettuce, wet lettuce in the store,
and I would keep driving, on and on.

California

Shouldn't we finally get started?
I mean I think the right time has come.
The wind drops the leaves to the ground.
I think we had better get going.
The sunrise, the sunrise has fallen.
The long rows of waves keep on coming.
They lap in the rocks by the shore.

I mean it is dusk on the shore.
And the wind kicks the leaves to the ground.
All over the black leaves are falling.
Why do we still only stand here?
The time for our starting has come.
Let us go to the boats and launch out;
I think it would be best to run.

What I mean is the sunrise is gone.
Let us run to the boats and start rowing.
The leaves, the leaves keep on falling.
The black leaves have covered the beaches.
And why do we still only stand here?
I mean why do we still only stand here?

is like a dull dream. From time to time
the paper boy comes grinning with proof that
something has happened after all. Here
where the highways end. To go north
from here, you must be a bird or wealthy.
The prospectors have each been starved and strained
away down southward and to old folks homes.
Here is where the nights end too. Never
to sense the dark for days is strange, and not
so hot as one might think. It is strange
always to be able to see, and say:
that is there and that is there and that
is over there, always. Strange, not to tell
the end of days by any other way
than clocks, and meals; televisions turning off.
Different, for things to seem
to the eyes like one day, that somehow
has slowed down to months, years, icebergs
of minutes so separated by an absence
from anything that ever came before,
that the anxious people find themselves
waiting for the swish on their lime lawns
of the dirty tennis shoes of
the grinning paper boy who brings them yesterday.

Mammoth Poem

A mammoth in a snowstorm
Fell down and broke his leg. Then
Fallen there he knew no thing to do.
Pain, and other weights, made
Those hairy shoulders heave until
The cold came tumbling, tumbling down . . .

Ah, but that's OK, mammoth.
Console yourself with this:
Someday, a bald-headed man
With wire-rimmed glasses
Will slice your belly wide; and find
Flowers! Pine Cones! Green!
What a great affirmation
That green should last so long!
                                        Naturally,
Man would want a chance
To have a hand in all that.

. . . So the New York Explorers' Club
Flew down mammoth meat from
Alaska, where it was roasted
And served as hors d'oeuvres . . .

To a group of men dressed like penguins
And walking like them too.
What an honor for you, mammoth.
Just think of that!
Then the flowers, mountains, cones, clouds, and
All those mammoths still hid

Under tons and tons of ice,
Simply receded, backed away,
Saying to the no one who listened,
"It is ended."

           . . . Next morning,
It was reported in the *Times*
That those who tasted found it
Quite good, but a little strange.

61

The North Slope

Three months away from the word away from trees
and bushes hills newspapers women dark
on into the undeodorized the raw
twelve hours a day seven days a week
helicopters dropped us on tundra unrelieved
abandoned well sites to do away with
anything "environmentally unsound" there that
first day stacking scrap metal thinking the last words
of Scarlett O'Hara seeing how flat
the land was how brown how completely
unrelieved the flatness how raw the air
coming off the Arctic Sea the horizon
a pencil line sometimes blending
with the frigid summer sky unrelieved
a foot and a half of tundra and under it
ice going down frozen earth eighteen hundred feet
I remember the small tundra flowers
delicate white blue the yellow poppies
in the second week I reached out to pick some
saw a jut of ice beside them
reaching up strange I shivered strange
something there I did not quite understand
could not get my mind around something
ice underneath them then back at base camp
before bed thought again and again
coldness what is it I thought strange unrelieved
more and more could not look at the flat
horizon or would not would keep my gaze away
from the white sky white fog the white
light from the sun never sinking what is it

I did not know only this feeling
someone walking always away something unsaid
and I kept my head down away from the sun the sky
then came the week of the caribou
the herds they came running unrelieved
thousands and thousands across the tundra
I kept my head down but at last could not
a hundred yards away two wolves loping behind
I saw them drag down a slow one
it was one hundred yards away
I saw them could not believe saw them
the red meadow of its side this was
one hundred yards away watched them eat
there was ice underground is ice
underground could not believe saw them rip ice
from its side ice the color of the sun I saw
it was raw it was nothing that fell from
its side ice emptiness came loping as birds
so many birds flew away and away screaming over
something they seemed to have heard
unrelieved the sound now of blood falling
of ice now and of whaleboats I could not believe
thinking her last words what was it the birds said
going away what was it the ice whispered raw
could not lift my head
the jet trails sagged over Dead Horse
and drifted away here where you aim
the harpoon sailor see it surface see it wallow
unrelieved see it dive here where the wait is
the ache for anything anything not dropping away
she breaches she breaches they cried and that
image charging my head all that white reaching

up that vacuum revealed unrelieved
and the froth all the spray and it sinking back
under leaving me asking for some other thing
for some other way asking time
to turn to forget what is there what is not
everywhere birds kept flying away
but Scarlett Scarlett this is the place
where tomorrow never comes the sun like
red ice searing always the summer the land
of absence of nothing of cold of no night
the wind blowing frozen off the Arctic Sea

The Polar Bear

In the only land where things are truly white,
The polar bear is too.
                    He lumbers about,
His round, white stomach full of fish.
The meat of the fish lies white inside him;
His thick, shaggy coat shines white in the sun.
And as he moves over snow and ice,
He slips out of sight before our eyes
In an almost magical blending of light.

And the polar bear has this land to himself.
All to himself he roams the ice;
For very few creatures, and fewer men,
Can live with the always unbending of white.

Like no man I know of, he sleeps at night
With his stomach, and dreams, full of white.

To His Book

Wafer; thin and hard and bitter pill I
   Take from time to time; pillow I have lain
      Too long on; holding the brief dreams, the styled
Dreams, the nightmares, shadows, red flames high
   High up on mountains; wilted zinnias, rain
      On dust, and great weight, the dead dog, and wild
Onions; mastodonic woman who knows how,—
   I'm tired of you, tired of your insane
      Acid eating in the brain. Sharp stones, piled
Particularly, I let you go. Sink, or float, or fly now,
               Bad child.